Hares

Copyright © 1981 by W.H. Allen & Co. Ltd.
Distributor's ISBN 0-312-92284-1
Publisher's ISBN 0-86553-030-0
Published by Congdon & Lattès, Inc.
Distributed by St. Martin's Press
All Rights Reserved
Picture research by D. Wyn Hughes and Fiona Hughes
Printed in the United States of America
First American Edition

Hares

**Edited by
D. Wyn Hughes**

CONGDON & LATTÈS
New York

'the mervellest beest that is on any londe'.

> DAME JULIANA BERNERS
> THE BOKE OF ST ALBANS

Amongst all Birds none with the Thrush
　　compare,
And no Beast hath more glory than the Hare.

> C. E. HARE
> THE LANGUAGE OF SPORT

n babilone vont ⁊ muevent
quant il furent montes ⁊
esquier de lost ont tout ar
grant ioie cheuauchent les

St Agnes' Eve? Ah, bitter chill it was!
The owl, for all his feathers, was a-cold;
The hare limp'd trembling through the frozen
    grass,
And silent was the flock in woolly fold.

                                      JOHN KEATS
                            From THE EVE OF ST AGNES

Here lies, whom hound did ne'er pursue,
    Nor swifter greyhound follow,
Whose foot ne'er tainted morning dew,
    Nor ear heard huntsman's halloo.

Old Tiney, surliest of his kind,
    Who, nursed with tender care,
And to domestic bounds confined,
    Was still a wild Jack hare.

A Turkey carpet was his lawn,
    Whereon he loved to bound,
To skip and gambol like a fawn,
    And swing his rump around.

Eight years and five round rolling moons,
    He thus saw steal away,
Dozing out all his idle noons,
    And every night at play.

I kept him for his humour's sake,
    For he would oft beguile
My heart of thoughts that made it ache,
    And force me to a smile.

WILLIAM COWPER
From EPITAPH ON A HARE

There was a table set out under a tree in front of the house, and the March Hare and the Hatter were having tea at it: a Dormouse was sitting between them, fast asleep, and the other two were using it as a cushion resting their elbows on it, and talking over its head. 'Very uncomfortable for the Dormouse,' thought Alice; 'only as it's asleep, suppose it doesn't mind.'

The table was a large one, but the three were all crowded together at one corner of it. 'No room! No room!' they cried out when they saw Alice coming. 'There's plenty of room!' said Alice indignantly, and she sat down in a large armchair at one end of the table.

'Have some wine,' the March Hare said in an encouraging tone.

Alice looked round the table, but there was nothing on it but tea. 'I don't see any wine,' she remarked.

'There isn't any,' said the March Hare.

'Then it wasn't very civil of you to offer it,' said Alice angrily.

'It wasn't very civil of you to sit down without being invited,' said the March Hare.

LEWIS CARROLL
ALICE'S ADVENTURES IN WONDERLAND

Nature seems to have gifted the Hare with some singularly preservative properties, of which her diversified tintings offer a proof; these so harmoniously blend with the matters which surround her as to make her escape from all but the practised eye very common. It is not that she lies concealed by cover; on the contrary, she frequently forms on the loo side of a clod in a ploughed field, and yet, although so situated, her mass looks so shapeless that she is, by those not habituated to look for her, more frequently passed over than discovered. Her ears also are so mobile that she can take in sounds from every quarter; her eyes are never shut, and although she without doubt sleeps, yet her visual organs are so framed as never to be veiled, and her sleep is also so light as to instantaneously communicate through them and her ears the approach of danger. If discovered, her speed would in most cases save her from common foes; but she is assailed on one part by dogs artificially bred with superior scenting powers, or on the other with such as, though almost scentless, are fleet as the wind. Poor puss!!

BLAIR'S RURAL SPORTS
THE REASON WHY, NATURAL HISTORY

Why is the Hare so called? – It is suggested that the name arises from the declaration of Pliny that the Hare is the 'hairiest creature of all others'. It is not improbable that the noun is of the same origin as the verb to hare, and that the name was given to the animal because it is harried, or pursued by harriers.

THE REASON WHY, NATURAL HISTORY

All through the days of the Flood, the Devil tried to sink the Ark by making holes in it. Noah put in a plug every time. But at last he had no plugs left. He cut off the Hare's tail and stopped the last hole with that. When the Devil saw this he fled. But since then hares have no tail.

OSKAR DÄHNHARDT
NATURSAGEN

Inhuman man! curse on thy barb'rous art,
   And blasted be thy murder-aiming eye;
   May never pity soothe thee with a sigh,
Nor ever pleasure glad thy cruel heart!

Go live, poor wanderer of the wood and field!
   The bitter little that of life remains:
   No more the thickening brakes and verdant plains
To thee shall home, or food, or pastime yield.

Perhaps a mother's anguish adds its woe;
   The playful pair crowd fondly by thy side;
   Ah! helpless nurslings, who will now provide
That life a mother only can bestow!

Oft as by winding Nith I, musing, wait
   The sober eve, or hail the cheerful dawn,
   I'll miss thee sporting o'er the dewy lawn,
And curse the ruffian's aim, and morn thy hapless fate.

ROBERT BURNS
From ON SEEING A WOUNDED HARE LIMP BY ME
WHICH A FELLOW HAD JUST SHOT

The Hare is a short-lived animal, and is supposed rarely to exceed the term of seven or eight years. Its voice, which is seldom heard but in the distress of sudden surprise or when wounded, resembles the sharp cry of an infant. Its enemies are numerous and powerful. Every species of dog kind pursues it by instinct; the cat and the weasel tribes exercise all their arts to ensnare it, and the birds of prey, snakes, adders etc drive it from its form, particularly during the summer season; these, with the more destructive pursuits of mankind, contribute to thin the number of these animals, which from their prolific nature would otherwise multiply to an extravagant degree.

The flesh is now much prized for its peculiar flavour, as it was by the Romans; but it was forbidden to be eaten among the Jews, Mahometans, and Ancient Britons. The fur, until of late years, when silk became so generally used, was of great importance in the manufacture of hats; and in some parts of the continent it is also woven into cloth.

SAMUEL MAUNDER
THE TREASURY OF NATURAL HISTORY

ANECDOTE OF A HARE
WITH EIGHT LEGS

For two days I had been pursuing a hare. My dog always started her, but I could never hit her. I do not believe in magic, I have seen too many wonderful things in my day for that; but I own that this hare puzzled me.

Day after day I followed her, but my coursing was always in vain. At length I got near enough to shoot her: she fell, and what do you think I discovered, Gentlemen?

She had four feet on her back, as well as those on earth. When the four ordinary ones were tired, she turned over with the greatest ease, and fled on with her four fresh feet instead.

I never saw a hare like this one, and I should assuredly never have taken it without Diana's* assistance. It surpassed others of its race so much, that I feel sure I shall not be taxed with exaggeration in styling it unique.

* Baron Munchausen's wonderful hound

THE ADVENTURES OF BARON MUNCHAUSEN

So ends the old yeare, I bless God, with great joy to me, not only from my having made so good a yeare of profit, as having spent £420 and laid up £540 and upwards; but I bless God I never have been in so good a plight as to my health in so very cold weather as this is, nor indeed in any hot weather, these ten years, as I am at this day, and have been these four or five months. But I am at a great loss to know whether it be my hare's foote, or taking every morning a pill of turpentine, or my having left off the wearing of a gowne.

December 31st 1664

So homeward, on my way buying a hare and taking it home, which arose upon my discourse today with Mr Batten, in Westminster Hall, who showed me my mistake that my hare's foote hath not the joynt in it; and assures me he never had his cholique since he carried it about him: and it is a strange thing how fancy works, for I no sooner almost handled his foote but my belly began to loose and to break wind, and where I was in some pain yesterday and tother day and in fear of more today, I became very well, and so continue.

January 20th 1664–65

THE DIARY OF SAMUEL PEPYS

Hare, is a beast of venery, of the forest; peculiarly so termed in the second year of her age; in the first year she is called a leveret; and in the third a great hare. By old foresters the hare is called King of All Beasts of Venery.

There are four sorts of hares; some live in the mountains, some in the fields, some in marshes, and some everywhere, without any certain place of abode. The mountain hares are the swiftest; the field hares are not so nimble; and those of the marshes are the slowest; but the wandering hares are the most dangerous to follow, for they are so cunning in the ways and mazes of the fields, running up the hills and rocks, because by custom they know a nearer way; with other tricks, to the confusion of the dogs and discouragement of the hunters.

It is admirable to behold how every limb and member of this beast is composed for celerity.

HENRY JAMES PYE ESQ
THE SPORTSMAN'S DICTIONARY

It is astonishing what may be effected by constant exertion and continual tormenting even the most timid and untractable animals; for no one would readily believe that a hare could have been sufficiently emboldened to face a large concourse of spectators without expressing its alarm, and beat upon a tambourine in their presence; yet such a performance was put in practice not years back, and exhibited at Sadler's Wells; and, if I mistake not, in several other places in and about the metropolis. Neither is this whimsical spectacle a recent invention. A hare that beat the tabor is mentioned by Jonson, in his Comedy Batholomew Fayre, acted at the commencement of the 17th century; and a representation of the feat itself, taken from a drawing on a manuscript upwards of four hundred years old, in the Harleian Collection is given.

JOSEPH STRUTT
THE SPORTS AND PASTIMES OF THE PEOPLE OF ENGLAND

A Hare is a four-footed Beast of the Earth, which the Hebrews call Arnebet, in the feminine gender which word gave occasion to an opinion that all Hares were females, or at the least that the males bring forth young as well as females . . . The common sort of people suppose they are one year male, and another female. Men find in Hares certain little bladders filled with matter, and against rain Hares suck thereout a certain humour, and anoint their bodies all over therewith, and so are defended in time of rain.

The eating of Hares procureth sleep. A waistcoat made of Hares' skins straightens the bodies of young and old. The rennet being mingled with vinegar is drunk against poison; and also if a man or beast be anointed with it, no serpent, scorpion, spider or wild mouse, whose teeth are venomous, will venture to sting the body so anointed. The same being mingled with snails or any other shell-fish, which feed upon green herbs or leaves, draweth forth thorns, darts, arrows, or reeds out of the belly.

EDWARD TOPSELL
FOUR-FOOTED BEASTS

All things that love the sun are out of doors;
The sky rejoices in the morning's birth;
The grass is bright with rain-drops; on the
    moors
The hare is running races in her mirth;
And with her feet she from the plashy earth
Raises a mist; which, glittering in the sun,
Runs with her all the way, wherever she doth
    run.

                        WILLIAM WORDSWORTH
             From RESOLUTION AND INDEPENDENCE

Metamorphoses were, according to Isobel Gowdie, very common amongst them*, and the forms of crows, cats, hares, and other animals, were on such occasions assumed. In the hare shape Isobel herself had a bad adventure. She had been sent by the Devil to Auldearn, in that favourite disguise, with some message to her neighbours, but had the misfortune to meet Peter Papley of Killhill's servants going to labour, having his hounds with them. The hounds sprung on the disguised witch, 'and I' says Isobel, 'run a very long time, but being hard pressed, was forced to take to my own house, the door being open, and there took refuge behind a chest'. But the hounds came in, and took the other side of the chest, so that Isobel only escaped by getting into another house, and gaining time to say the disenchanting rhyme:–

> Hare, hare, God send thee care!
> I am in a hare's likeness now;
> But I shall be woman even now –
> Hare, hare, God send thee care!

* The Witches of Auldearn

SIR WALTER SCOTT
DEMONOLOGY AND WITCHCRAFT

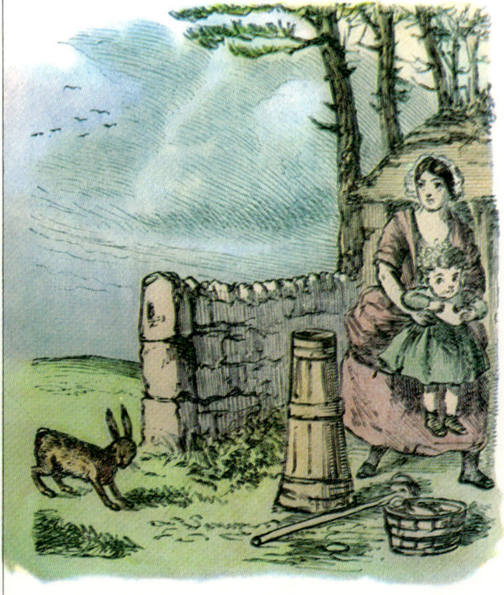

Bluey's delight was to jump on to the bed and play on the eiderdown coverlet, which she seemed to take as her native heather. Placing herself in the middle, she would leap into the air, fling herself round, make a rush at me as I stood on one side, and then retire to the centre as to a stronghold, whence she defied all the world. When I returned to my study, she would come galloping in, approach my chair, and then rush out, repeating this performance over and over again. At other times she would jump on the dressing table and sit pensively for a long while opposite the looking glass.

REV. RICHARD WILTON
NATURAL HISTORY NOTES AND ANECDOTES

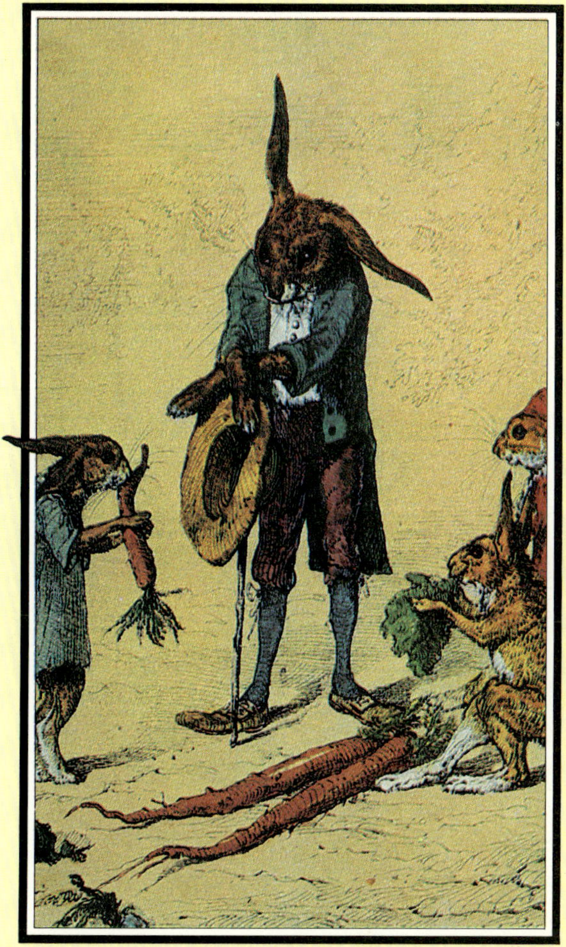

The Hare is so pleasing, that whoever sees it either trailed, or found, or pursued, or taken, forgets every 'thing else he is most attached to'.

Xenophon

HENRY JAMES PYE ESQ
THE SPORTSMAN'S DICTIONARY

With its brains boys' gums are cleansed; for it has the property to make the teeth come quickly, and without pain. Its head burnt with bear's grease, and used as a plaster, helps baldness.

H. W. SEAGER
NATURAL HISTORY IN SHAKESPEARE'S TIME

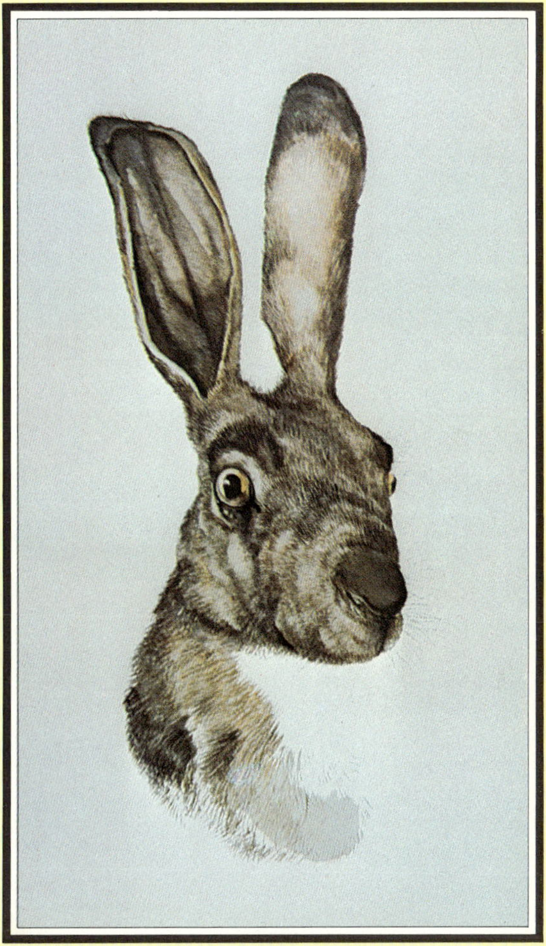

There is a great lake abounding in water, called Chandrasaras (Moon Lake), and on its banks lived a king of the hares, Silimukha. Now, once on a time, a leader of a herd of elephants, named Chaturdanta, came to drink water . . . many of the hares, who were subjects of the king, were trampled to death by Chaturdanta's herd, while entering the lake.

A wise hare said to the elephant: 'I am the ambassador of the Moon, and this is what the God says to you by my mouth: "I dwell in a cool lake named Chandrasaras; there dwell hares whose king I am, and I love them well . . . now thou hast defiled that lake and slain those hares of mine. If thou doest that again, thou shall receive thy due recompense from me."'

When the king of the elephants heard this speech of the crafty hare he said in his terror, 'I will never do it again: I must show respect to the awful moon-god.' The hare said: 'So come, my friend, I will show him to you' . . . and showed him the reflection of the moon in the water. When the lord of the herd saw that, he bowed before it . . . and never came there again.

G. H. TAWNEY *(Translator)*
THE ELEPHANTS AND THE HARES IN THE
OCEAN OF STORY

هاملاالاير فأوى عندها   فلماسمع ذلك الفيل اعجبه فانطلق
فاراه ظل القمر ففعل الفيل ذلك فاضطرب الماء وتحرك ظل القمر فيه فقال نظر
غضبه فقلت تخوف ذلك واشفق منه وما استطاع لاحدمنا الفيله
صورة الفيل غاطس فى العين ظل القمر العين والارنب مرتفعة تنظر وتخاف

وانماضربت لكم هذا المثل لان النوم سريع الغب شديد لايستطاع
الدنى منه الا المشاورة له بجنون وحلم وهن شن وتمسك بالملك ولا

The feet of a Hare together with the stone otherwise the head of an ousel move a man to boldness, so that he fears not death. And if it be bound on the left arm, he will go whither he will, and return safely without danger. And if it be given to a dog to eat with the heart of a weasel, he will make no noise from thenceforth, even if he is being killed.

ALBERTUS MAGNUS
OF VIRTUES OF ANIMALS

47

THE HARE AND THE TORTOISE

A Hare insulted a Tortoise upon account of his slowness, and vainly boasted of his own great speed in running.

'Let us make a match,' replied the Tortoise. 'I'll run with you five miles for five pounds, and the Fox yonder shall be the umpire of the race.'

The Hare agreed, and away they both started together. But the Hare, by reason of his exceeding swiftness, outran the Tortoise to such a degree that he made a jest of the matter, and finding himself a little tired, squatted in a tuft of fern that grew by the way and took a nap; thinking, that if the Tortoise went by, he could at any time catch him up with all the ease imaginable. In the meanwhile the Tortoise came jogging on with a slow but continued motion, and the Hare, out of too great a security and confidence of victory, oversleeping himself, the Tortoise arrived at the end of the race first.

Keeping on wins the race.

AESOP'S FABLES

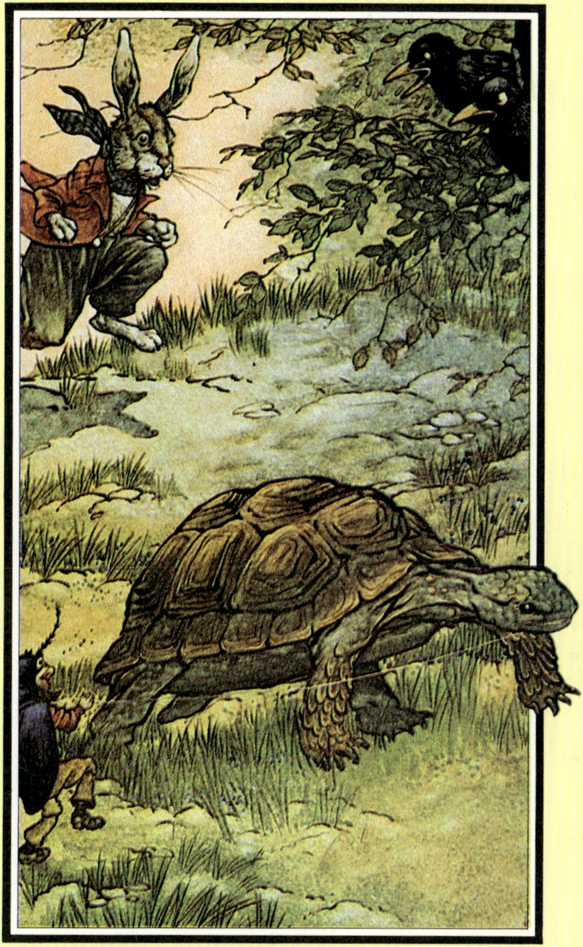

The Hare first taught us the use of the herbe called wyld succory, which is very excellent for those which are disposed to be malancholicke. She herselfe is one of the most melancholicke beasts that is, and to heale her own infirmitie, she goeth commonly to sit under that hearbe.

GEORGE TURBERVILLE
THE BOOK OF HUNTING

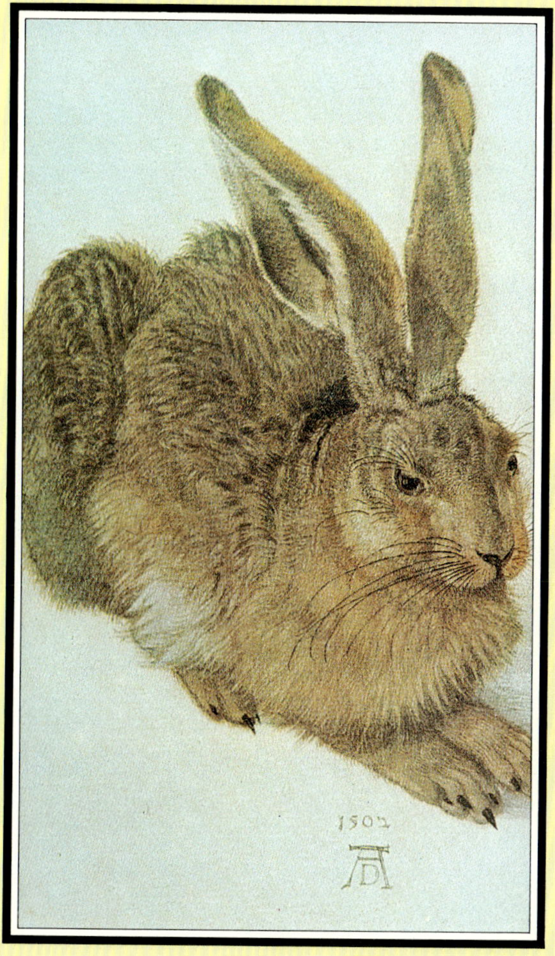
1502

At no other coursing ground which I have visited was the percentage of kills so small; but Puss had one big pull in her favour, and this often gave her a means of escape when she was hard pressed. It was as follows.

The enclosure was divided by stone walls, built up to a great height, and at intervals small holes had been made at the bottom of the walls (these are called smouts). Puss knew these places, and invariably bolted through when she got a chance, the greyhounds were unable to follow, but often struggled for a moment at the hole before drawing back and leaping the wall. This of course allowed the hare a second law, and she would often double down the side of the wall and take advantage of the next 'smout' to return into the original field. A certain fluky element was thus introduced into High Law* coursing; but that was of no account with the farmers, whose sympathies, by the way, were mostly with the hare, and who were better pleased if she escaped, provided she had given their dogs a fair course before she eluded them.

* Name of the farm: High Law Farm

CHARLES RICHARDSON
COURSING THE HARE

53

Illustration acknowledgements

5 Hare Hunting Man. 14th century Flemish. Ms Bodley 264 FS 93–17

7 Archibald Thorburn. *Thorburn's Mammals*. Ebury Press & Michael Joseph

9 William Cowper in his Garden. *Lady Aberconway's Dictionary of Cat Lovers*. Michael Joseph.

11 Arthur Rackham. 'Mad Tea Party', *Alice in Wonderland*. Lewis Carroll. William Heinemann.

13 Archibald Thorburn. *Thorburn's Mammals*. Ebury Press & Michael Joseph

15 Hare and Horse. 16th century. *English Herbal & Bestiary*. Ms Ashmole 1504. FS 156B 66

17 John Leech. *Ask Mamma*. Robert Smith Surtees. Bradbury Agnew & Co.

19 Harp and Hare. Ms Ashmole 1525. FB FS 187J–6

21 Land of Burns. George Virtue. 1838

23 E. J. Detmold. *Fables of Aesop*. Hodder & Stoughton

25 A. Bichard. *The Adventures of Baron Munchausen*. Frederick Warne & Co.

27 Patrick Oxenham. The Post Office

29 Chinese scroll on silk. *Circa* 1700. *The Book of Hunting*. Paddington Press

31 Hare and Tabor. *Sports and Pastimes of the People of England*. Joseph Strutt, 1834.

33 Kit Williams. *Masquerade*. Jonathan Cape

35 Hare and Hounds. Old Warden, Bedfordshire.

37 John Leech. *Ask Mamma*. Robert Smith Surtees. Bradbury, Agnew & Co.

39 Ernest Griset. *Grace Before Meat*. Victoria & Albert Museum. Crown Copyright

41 Peter Kettle. Head of Hare

43 Hare and the Moon. Ms Pockocke. F99R. Bodleian Library

45 Fiona Hughes. Leverets

47 Egyptian Antiquities. British Museum

49 Charles Folkard. *Aesop's Fables*. Adam & Charles Black

51 Albrecht Durer. Albertina Library, Vienna

53 C. Whymper. From 'Coursing the Hare' by Charles Richardson in *The Hare*. Longmans, Green & Co., 1903

For permission to use copyright material we are indebted to the following:

Frederick Warne and Co. for an excerpt from *The Adventures of Baron Munchausen*; and Country Life Ltd for a quote from Frances Pitt's *Romance of Nature*.

Editor's acknowledgements and thanks to Amanda Girling, Mike Brett and the Secker Family.